This book belongs to

EDEN and
AGAM
•••••••••••••••••••••••••••••••••••••

Benluc

This is a Parragon Publishing Book
This edition published in 2006

Parragon Publishing
Queen Street House
4 Queen Street
Bath BA1 1HE, UK

Copyright © Parragon Books Ltd 2001

Created by small world creations ltd
Printed in China
ISBN 1-40545-358-3

A First Counting Book

p

1 one

1 cuddly teddy bear...

...to hug!

2 two

2 smiling twins...

...wearing pretty party hats!

3 three

3 juicy apples...

...to crunch and munch!

4 four

4 birthday candles...

...for blowing out!

5 five

5 playful puppies...

...playing catch in the park.

6 six

6 yummy ice creams...

"...taste yummy in my tummy."

7 seven

7 perfect eggs...

...and 7 fluffy chicks!

8 eight

8 shiny beads...

...for making a necklace!

9 nine

9 squishy cakes...

...for a tasty treat!

10 ten

10 sticky fingers...

...to count with!

How many puppies can you count?

How many cakes can you see?

Can you find a Teddy Bear?

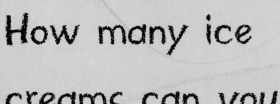
How many ice

creams can you count?

Now see if you can count from 1 to 10!